Sports Illustrated

STARS OF SPORTS

BUBBA WALLACE

STOCK CAR RACING STAR

by Lisa A. Crayton

Published by Capstone Press, an imprint of Capstone
1710 Roe Crest Drive
North Mankato, Minnesota 56003
capstonepub.com

SPORTS ILLUSTRATED KIDS is a trademark of ABG-SI LLC. Used with permission.

Library of Congress Cataloging-in-Publication Data
Names: Crayton, Lisa A., author. Title: Bubba Wallace : stock car racing star / by Lisa A. Crayton. Description: North Mankato, Minnesota : Capstone Press, [2022] | Series: Sports illustrated kids stars of sports | Includes bibliographical references and index. | Audience: Ages 8-11 | Audience: Grades 4-6 | Summary: "Bubba Wallace started racing cars at nine years old. He began competing in 2010 and hasn't slowed down since, setting records as the youngest winner at many races. He was the first Black driver to win Rookie of the Year for NASCAR. Find out how Wallace's talent has led him to success in the world of stock car racing" —Provided by publisher. Identifiers: LCCN 2021042154 (print) | LCCN 2021042155 (ebook) | ISBN 9781663983619 (hardcover) | ISBN 9781666323085 (paperback) | ISBN 9781666323092 (pdf) | ISBN 9781666323115 (kindle edition) Subjects: LCSH: Wallace, Bubba, 1993- —Juvenile literature. | Automobile racing drivers—United States—Biography—Juvenile literature. | African American athletes—United States—Biography—Juvenile literature. | NASCAR (Association)—History. Classification: LCC GV1032.W34 C73 2022 (print) | LCC GV1032.W34 (ebook) | DDC 796.720973 [B]—dc23 LC record available at https://lccn.loc.gov/2021042154 LC ebook record available at https://lccn.loc.gov/2021042155

Editorial Credits
Editor: Christianne Jones; Designer: Bobbie Nuytten; Media Researcher: Morgan Walters; Production Specialist: Laura Manthe

Image Credits
Associated Press: Alex Menendez, 5, Brynn Anderson, 20, Chuck Burton, 23, John Raoux, 24, Rich Graessle/Icon Sportswire, 28, Richard W. Rodriguez, 25, Steve Helber, 21; Getty Images: Elsa, 13, 15, Robert Laberge, 27, Rusty Jarrett, 11, 12; Newscom: David Allio/Icon SMI 951, 4, David J. Griffin/Icon SMI 953, 9, John Cordes/Icon Sportswire 506, 17, Justin R. Noe Asp Inc/ZUMA Press, Cover; Shutterstock: Avigator Fortuner, 1, Gary Krieg, 8, Joseph Sohm, 7

Source Notes
Page 5, "I just try . . . " Michelle R. Martinelli, "Bubba Wallace celebrates 2nd-place Daytona 500 finish with tears and hug from his mom," USA Today, February 18, 2018, https://ftw.usatoday.com/2018/02/darrell-bubba-wallace-jr-nascar-daytona-500-austin-dillon-emotional-press-conference-video, Accessed September 7, 2021.
Page 19, "I'm seeing . . . " Michelle R. Martinelli, "Bubba Wallace reflects on reaching his 'breaking point' and the challenges of being NASCAR's lone Black voice," USA Today, February 10, 2021, https://ftw.usatoday.com/2021/02/nascar-bubba-wallace-michael-jordan-hamlin-voice-diversity-daytona-500, Accessed September 7, 2021.
Page 19, "I didn't set . . . " Chris Estrada, "Bubba Wallace named NMPA Pocono Spirit Award winner," NBC Sports, January 25, 2021, https://nascar.nbcsports.com/2021/01/25/nascar-cup-series-bubba-wallace-nmpa-pocono-spirit-award-winner/, Accessed September 7, 2021.
Page 19, ". . . we're just trying . . . " Justin Kirkland, "Bubba Wallace is NASCAR's Future and the Future is Now," Esquire, October 4, 2020, https://www.esquire.com/sports/a34210910/bubba-wallace-profile-return-to-talladega/, Accessed September 7, 2021.
Page 21, "I never thought . . . " Bubba Wallace, "Come Ride With Me," The Players' Tribune, July 16, 2020, https://www.theplayerstribune.com/articles/bubba-wallace-nascar-racism/, Accessed September 7, 2021.
Page 22, "I have very good . . . " Dustin Long, "Michael Jordan excited for NASCAR future with Denny Hamlin," NBC Sports, September 23, 2020, https://nascar.nbcsports.com/2020/09/23/michael-jordan-denny-hamlin-excited-for-nascar-partnership/, Accessed September 7, 2021.
Page 26, "It all goes away . . . " Associated Press, "NASCAR: Bubba Wallace admits he's struggling with depression," May 10, 2019, The Tennessean, https://www.tennessean.com/story/sports/2019/05/10/bubba-wallace-depression-nascar-monster-energy-cup-series/1170342001/, Accessed September 7, 2021.

All internet sites appearing in back matter were available and accurate when this book was sent to press.

TABLE OF CONTENTS

Words in **BOLD** are in the glossary.

A FANTASTIC FINISH

The final lap of the 2018 Daytona 500 grew close to an end. Bubba Wallace was in car number 43. He was the first Black driver in the event since Wendell Scott in 1969. Wallace lagged behind three other **NASCAR** drivers. His dream of winning the event for the first time was out of reach. But the finish line was in sight. Wallace kept flying along the track.

>>> Wendell Scott was the first Black NASCAR driver.

>>> Wallace speeds around the track during the Daytona 500 race in 2018.

Suddenly, the lead car spun out, Austin Dillon took over and finished in first place. Moments later, Wallace edged ahead of Denny Hamlin. The result? A second-place finish! "I just try so hard to be successful at everything I do," Wallace said through tears during an interview after the race.

FACT

Wallace is only the second Black driver in the NASCAR Cup Series.

CHAPTER ONE
FLYING START

William Darrell Wallace Jr. was born on October 8, 1993, in Mobile, Alabama. His 5-year-old sister, Brittany, gave her baby brother the nickname "Bubba." Soon everyone called him Bubba. Wallace is **biracial**. His father is white. His mother is Black.

When Wallace was 2 years old, the family moved to Concord, North Carolina. Concord is less **diverse** than where Wallace was born. Fewer Black people live in Concord. The move changed their lives. It introduced the family to **stock car** racing. The sport is very popular in Concord. The city is home to Charlotte Motor Speedway. It hosts NASCAR races.

⟩⟩⟩ An aerial view of Charlotte Motor Speedway in Concord, North Carolina

NO MORE HOOPS

Growing up, Wallace and his sister played basketball. His interests took a turn at age 9 when his father bought him a go-kart. Go-karts are similar to small race cars. Wallace loved the sport. He quit playing basketball. Wallace traces his love for fast driving to his early go-kart days.

Although go-karts are fast, Bandoleros are faster. These small cars look like miniature stock cars. They can travel more than 60 miles (97 kilometers) per hour. That is faster than the speed limit on some highways!

Wallace moved on to racing Bandoleros and even faster cars. He started entering competitions. He was the only Black driver.

>>> A Bandolero race at the Bullring at Las Vegas Motor Speedway

>>> Wallace and his team cheer after winning the Kroger 200 Camping World Truck Series race in 2013.

Racing to the Top

Wallace has competed in NASCAR's Camping World Truck Series, Xfinity Series, and Cup Series. The different levels mark a driver's experience. The Truck Series is where drivers gain experience before moving on to the Xfinity Series. The Xfinity Series is like the "minor leagues" for drivers. If they are successful there, they can move up to the top-level Cup Series.

CHAPTER TWO

IN THE FAST LANE

Stock car racing is a sport that attracts mostly white drivers. The majority of fans also are white. Wallace stood out because he is Black. When he was young, he heard a racial slur at an event. It happened again at about age 14 when a couple of individuals got mad at the way Wallace drove.

Wallace was shocked! He had not focused on the fact he was the only Black racer. He simply concentrated on competing. The name-calling got his attention. Wallace's mother told him that he had to decide if other people's actions would stop him. Mostly, she encouraged him to keep driving and to win.

FACT

NASCAR's Drive for Diversity program continues to help new drivers. Rajah Caruth will make his debut in the 2022 Xfinity Series, making him the second Black driver in NASCAR today.

Wallace continued his love of stock car racing. He stayed in the driver's seat. His driving took a positive turn in 2010. He was selected for NASCAR's Drive for Diversity program. This training program helps women drivers and minorities improve their skills and get more experience. The program also helps train them to become NASCAR **pit crew** members.

⟩⟩⟩ Wallace (right) participating in a press conference for NASCAR's Drive for Diversity program

A HELPING HAND

Wallace graduated from the Drive for Diversity program. Being part of it moved him closer to his goal of becoming a professional stock car racer. Drivers usually start at regional events. If they continue to do well, they move up to national events.

Wallace entered NASCAR regional competitions in the K&N Pro Series East. He got off to a great start, winning his first race! That victory made him the series' youngest winning driver ever. Wallace won other races. He attracted attention as a rising NASCAR driver. He was named the 2010 K&N Pro Series East **Rookie** of the Year.

》》》 Wallace (second from right) poses with other NASCAR Drive for Diversity participants

>>> Wallace celebrating after his K&N Pro Series East win

CHAPTER THREE

MOVING UP

In May 2012, 18-year-old Wallace made his **debut** in the NASCAR Xfinity Series. A year later, Wallace entered the Truck Series races. He won his first event in October 2013. He raced into history as the first Black driver to win a NASCAR national series race in 50 years!

In 2013 and 2014, Wallace's Truck Series skills attracted attention. His speeds were impressive, placing him among the fastest drivers. During 2015 and 2016, he was among the top-10 drivers in many Xfinity Series events. In the 2015 Xfinity Series, he finished seventh in the final points standings. In 2016, he finished 11th.

>>> Wallace crossing the finish line in first place during a NASCAR K&N Pro Series East race

FACT

The 2017 animated *Cars 3* movie features Wallace as the voice of Bubba Wheelhouse, the number 6 Piston Cup race car.

A FAMOUS RIDE

In 2017, Wallace raced in both the Xfinity and Truck Series. Soon he got a big break. Aric Almirola, a driver for Richard Petty Motorsports (RPM), injured his back and a new driver was needed. Wallace got the opportunity to drive for RPM. It was a big deal. Wallace would drive in the top-level Cup Series for Richard Petty. Petty is a NASCAR Cup Series legend. He has the most NASCAR race wins ever with 200.

Wallace drove Petty's number 43 car. Although he did not win for RPM in 2017, he kept improving. Petty offered Wallace a full-time job as a driver. Wallace accepted and became only the second Black driver who has raced full time in NASCAR's top series.

Wallace made history again in 2018. He became the first Black driver to compete in the Daytona 500 in 49 years. He finished in second place! It was the highest finish by a rookie full-time driver in the event. When the season ended, he had three top-10 finishes.

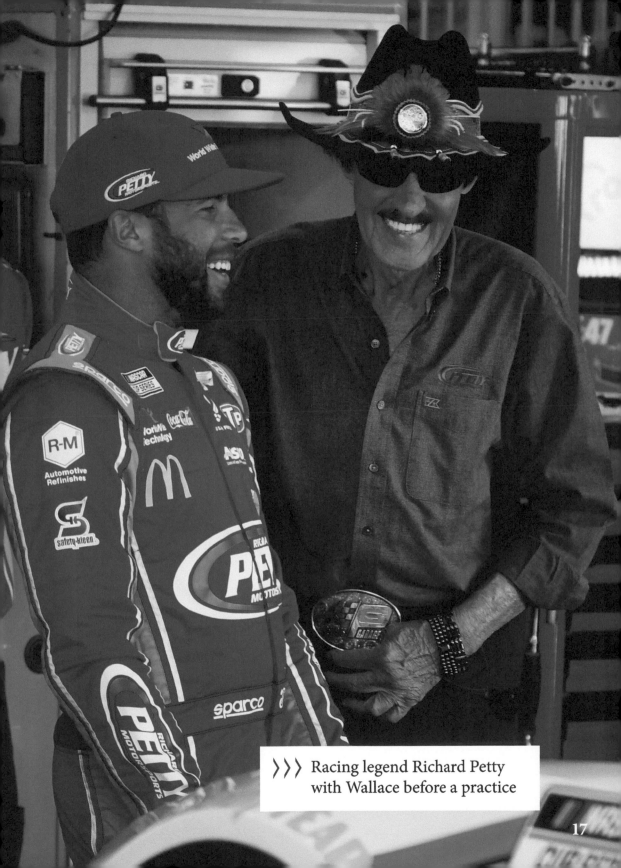

⟩⟩⟩ Racing legend Richard Petty with Wallace before a practice

CHAPTER FOUR

DRIVING CHANGE

The **COVID-19** pandemic brought NASCAR to a screeching halt in 2020. But first, it was racing as usual. Wallace had one of his best finishes at the Pennzoil 400 at the Las Vegas Motor Speedway in February. Soon after, NASCAR **suspended** all races.

When NASCAR started back up in May, Wallace was ready to race. Then two videos captured his attention. One was the Ahmaud Arbery killing in Georgia in February. Then Wallace saw the video of a police officer killing George Floyd during an arrest in Minnesota in May. These videos made Wallace rethink his fame.

In an interview Wallace said, "I'm seeing everything that's going on in the world, the innocent killings, and it was just like, 'Alright, it's time for me to say something.' People are asking for my opinion—not that my opinion matters—but they still want to know what the only Black driver has to say."

In receiving an award in 2021 partly for his **activism**, Wallace said, "I didn't set out to become an advocate this year, but as things were happening around our country, I found myself in a position to use my voice and push for change. I'm proud of what we accomplished, but we still have work today."

Black Lives Matter

Protests after the George Floyd killing brought the Black Lives Matter movement to the forefront. Its overall message is one of social justice and **equality**. In a show of support, Wallace's car had #BlackLivesMatter painted on it for a race. He also wore a T-shirt in support of the movement. Not interested in getting involved with the politics of the incident, Wallace explained, ". . . we're just trying to say we're all equal."

A TENSE SUMMER

Protests broke out in the summer of 2020 to spotlight the need for reform in police forces. Wallace pushed for change in a different way. He successfully called for a ban of Confederate flags at NASCAR races.

>>> Wallace supporting the Black Lives Matter movement

The Confederate Flag

The Confederate flag is associated with the American Civil War (1861–1865) when the Union and the Confederate states fought. The Confederacy, made up of 11 southern states, favored the enslavement of Black people. The Confederacy used several flags to represent itself, had its own president, and more. The Union's victory reunited the states. But more than a 150 years later people still flew the Confederate flag, and often at NASCAR events.

>>> The #BlackLivesMatter car that Wallace unveiled in June 2020

In light of the racial tension during the summer, Wallace felt removing the flags would be a positive step. His activism attracted a lot of attention—both positive and negative. But because of Wallace, the flags are no longer permitted at NASCAR races. "I never thought I'd be the reason for a national media debate about the Confederate flag," Wallace wrote in an essay.

Even while supporting his beliefs, Wallace still focused on driving in 2020. He raced his way to five top-10 finishes, a career high. He finished 22nd in the points standings, a solid improvement from 2019.

Wallace switched gears after the 2020 season. He left RPM and joined the newly formed 23XI (pronounced twenty-three eleven) Racing. It is a single-car team and Wallace is its only driver. The team started racing in 2021.

The 23XI Racing co-owners are three-time Daytona 500 winner Denny Hamlin and basketball legend Michael Jordan. Hamlin brings NASCAR experience to the partnership, while Jordan is a long-time fan.

About their new team Hamlin said in an interview, "I have very good faith that Bubba is going to have everything that he needs to be capable of winning, and I think he's got the talent to do it."

〉〉〉 Michael Jordan practices waving the green flag before a NASCAR All-Star race.

FACT

The 23XI team name combines Michael Jordan's basketball jersey number with Denny Hamlin's race car number.

Wallace made his team debut at the 2021 Daytona 500 driving the number 23 car. He led on lap 129 and became the first Black driver to lead a lap in the race. On June 27, he secured 23XI's first top-five finish at Pocono Raceway.

〉〉〉 Wallace gets back into his car after a weather delay at the Daytona 500 in 2021.

Off-Track Honors

Wallace's achievements are not limited to the racetrack. He has received recognition for his activism and other efforts. The awards he received in 2020 include the Stan Musial Award for Extraordinary Character, the Comcast Community Champion of the Year Award, and the National Motorsports Press Association Pocono Spirit Award.

DARING TO BE DIFFERENT

Being a race-car driver is a dream come true for Wallace. Racing is not just fun for him. It also helps him deal with depression. Depression negatively affects people's minds and bodies. It affects people's eating and sleep habits and causes other challenges.

In an interview before a race in May 2019, Wallace said he has faced the mental health condition for many years but hid it. "It all goes away when you get behind the wheel. . . . It helps. But it's tough," he said.

Wallace is not satisfied with his own success. He wants to help other people achieve their goals. He started the Live to Be Different Foundation in 2017. It offers a variety of support to people who are disadvantaged through a message of compassion, love, and understanding.

>>> Wallace (back row, left) and a group of other NASCAR drivers pose with the Xfinity Series trophy after the 2016 Drive for Safety 300.

Wallace is pushing for change in NASCAR. Only time will tell how much his spectacular driving, activism, and support for a more-inclusive sport will have in the stock car racing community. In the meantime he's doing what he loves—driving fast!

〉〉〉 Wallace races around the track in a 2021 NASCAR Cup Series race.

TIMELINE

1993 William Darrell "Bubba" Wallace Jr. is born on October 8 in Mobile, Alabama.

1995 Wallace moves with his family to Concord, North Carolina, where NASCAR is popular.

2002 Wallace starts racing go-karts.

2010 Wallace is named Rookie of the Year in the NASCAR K&N Pro Series East.

2012 Wallace begins competing in the NASCAR Xfinity Series.

2013 Wallace becomes the first Black driver to win a NASCAR national series race in 50 years.

2017 Wallace begins driving the number 43 car for Richard Petty Motorsports.

2018 Wallace finishes in second place at the Daytona 500.

2020 Wallace helps get Confederate flags banned at NASCAR races.

2021 Wallace begins driving for 23XI Racing.

GLOSSARY

ACTIVISM (AK-tuh-viz-uhm)—taking actions to bring change

BIRACIAL (bahy-REY-shuuhl)—involves people of two races

COVID-19 (KOH-vid nine-TEEN)—a very contagious and sometimes deadly virus that spread worldwide in 2020

DEBUT (DEY-byoo)—first public showing

DIVERSE (dih-VURS)—having different qualities, such as people of different races

EQUALITY (ih-KWOL-i-tee)—the same rights for everyone

NASCAR (NAS-kahr)—stands for the National Association for Stock Car Auto Racing

PIT CREW (PIT KROO)—a team who quickly fixes tires, adds fuel, makes repairs, and performs other duties to get a car back in a race

ROOKIE (ROOK-ee)—an athlete playing their first season as a member of a professional team

STOCK CAR (STOK KAHR)—a car modified for racing at high speeds

SUSPEND (suh-SPEND)—to temporarily stop

READ MORE

Goldsworthy, Steve. *The Tech Behind Race Cars.*
North Mankato, MN: Capstone Press, 2019.

Reinke, Beth Bence. *Superfast Stock Car Racing.*
Minneapolis: Lerner Publishing Group, Inc., 2020.

Stratton, Connor. *Bubba Wallace: Auto Racing Star.*
Lake Elmo, MN: Focus Readers, 2021.

INTERNET SITES

Bubba Wallace
bubbawallace.com

NASCAR
nascar.com

23XI Racing
23xiracing.com

INDEX

AUTHOR BIO

Lisa A. Crayton has written fifteen books for kids and teens and co-authored six others. She loves coaching writers, and especially enjoys speaking at writers' conferences. She is a member of the Society of Children Book Writers & Illustrators, the American Society of Journalists and Authors, Evangelical Press Association, and Alpha Kappa Alpha Sorority (service).